MACKINAC ISLAND

Three Hundred Fifty Years of History

by

Robert E. Benjamin

Contents

Published by Benjamin of Mackinac Island, Michigan 49757

INTRODUCTION

This history will aid the visitors in their enjoyment of Mackinac Island by sketching the historical background of the Island. A complete history in this small space is not possible but effort has been made to attest to the accuracy of the facts presented. I have arranged the contents chronologically and have placed important dates and points of interest in large type for easy reference. A number of suggested walks and bicycle rides are included for the convenience of the visitor with only a few hours to spend at Mackinac.

Fort Michilimackinac at Mackinaw City in the early pioneer days

Places of Interest to Mackinac Island Visitors

Information about the points of interest can be found by referring to the page number following the item These items are shown in bold face in the text.

Mackinac Island Michigan

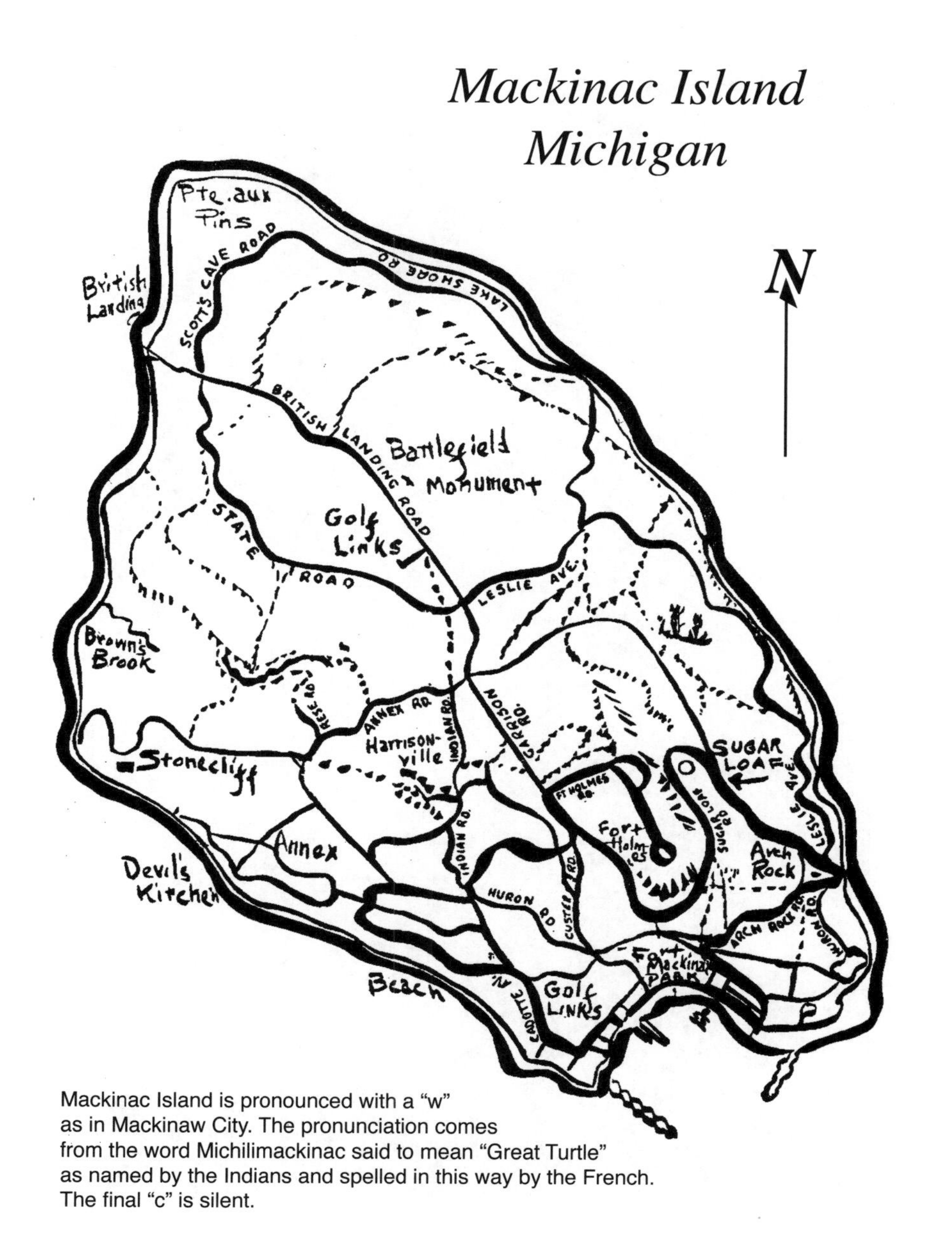

Mackinac Island is pronounced with a "w"
as in Mackinaw City. The pronunciation comes
from the word Michilimackinac said to mean "Great Turtle"
as named by the Indians and spelled in this way by the French.
The final "c" is silent.

Arch Rock, formed by the retreating waters of the glacial ice cap, stands 149 feet above the level of the Straits of Mackinac.

INDIAN LEGENDS OF MACKINAC ISLAND

GITCHIE MANITOU was chief and Great Spirit of all the Indians, and he created Mackinac Island, according to Indian legend. After calling into existence the beautiful island, legend says, the Manitou gave it into the care of the kindred spirits of earth, air and water, telling them that it was to be the abode of peace and quiet. Mackinac Island was so peaceful in his eyes that he thought, “Here will I also come to dwell, this shall be my abode and my children may come and worship me here. Here in the depths of the beautiful forest they shall come.”

CALLING his messengers, the great Manitou bade them fly to all lands of heat and noise and troublous insects and tell the suffering ones of every race and clime that in these northern waters was a place prepared where they could come and rest, leaving all care behind. The cool invigorating breezes shall bring health and elasticity to the weak and weary,” the Manitou of legend says. “Here disease shall not dare invade the pleasant glens or beautiful hill tops. Here let them come and receive my blessing.

YE shall also tell the stranger friend, who may come to seek me, that my royal landing is on the Eastern Shore; there shall they draw up the canoes upon the pebbly beach under the shadow of the Arched Gateway. Under the Arch, which they can see from afar, let them come with songs of rejoicing—neither night nor day shall it be closed to anyone who may seek me. Let them land before it and pass through it and ascend to my dwelling and worship before me.”

Sugar Loaf rock rises 90 feet. Photo by Foley Brothers about 1890

When the Great Spirit made known his wish to dwell with men, all nature seemed to rejoice and to make preparations for his abode, legend says. The tallest trees claimed the privilege of being the poles of the wigwam, and the sweet balsam fir laid themselves at his feet for use. The birch trees unsheathed themselves and sent their bark in all its creamy whiteness to form the outside covering. The trees of the forest all vied with each other in seeking a place in the future home of the Gitchie Manitou. Scarcely had the poles fitted themselves into their places and the birch bark unrolled itself and arranged its clinging sheets in orderly rows upon the outside, when the noise of distant paddles was heard from the lake. Swiftly and gaily the canoes drew near, guided by the spirits of earth, air, and water. " Never had such a sight been witnessed on this earth."

GITCHIE MANITOU was chief and went to meet the visitors, and stood upon the arch and upheld his hands in blessing. His children unloaded their offerings of beaver, white bear and beaver skins and marched in procession up to the gateway. They fell upon their knees and offered their thanks to the great spirit for the happy privilege of contributing to the comforts of his earthly home.

"Yes, my children dear, my loved ones.
I am here in joy and gladness.
Here to live in peace among you
I have come to teach you wisdom
In the arts of love and living.
I accept your native offerings.
These white bear, and fox skins silvery.
Shall a couch of warmth and comfort
Make for me when around my fire,
I am resting from my labors.
Of the beaver skins and otters
They shall line the wigwam smoothly,

Manitou Trail—Photo probably by Gardner about 1895.

So Ka-bi-bo-nok-ka, the north wind,
Ne're shall whistle thru them.
Enter in my gate way proudly
And ascend my staircase slowly,
And see the home of the Great Spirit Where he dwells among his children."

Many, many years have passed and the wigwam of the Great Spirit has been transmuted into stone and is now known as **Sugar Loaf**, the Indian legend concludes.

Sugar Loaf is a lime stone formation, standing 79 feet above the road with its tip 284 feet above lake level. The arched gateway, now called **Arch Rock**, is much as the Indians first saw it, with its portals guarded by tall green sentinels. A large rock on the East Shore Boulevard at Mackinac today bears the name of Gitchie Manitou and marks the legendary spot where these children of the Great Manitou landed. Geologists say that this was probably once a part of Arch Rock which is directly above. No doubt Arch Rock was one of the first points on the island above water in ancient geological times and was formed by the action of the receding waters. The summit of the arch reaches 149 feet above Lake Huron, while the arch spans 50 feet.

Manitou Trail is one of the oldest on the Island and leads from Arch Rock along the edge of the east bluff to **Robertson's Folly**. This trail is named for the Manitous who in Indian mythology were supernatural beings of various kinds. There were local Manitous of streams, rocks, and forests which revealed themselves to man only in the form of some beast, bird or reptile. Every Indian chose his guardian Manitou at an early age usually under the influence of extreme fasting.

Encampment on the shore at Mackinac Island.

About **Robertson's Folly,** a rock formation over looking the lake on the east point of the island, one hears a legend originating after the white man's arrival on Mackinac. Captain Robertson served in the fort garrison for seven years and was its commandant from 1782 to 1787. One evening he was strolling behind the fort when he saw a dark haired maiden that he had not noticed on Mackinac before. When he asked her name, she only smiled and disappeared into the forest. He inquired about her in the village but no one knew her.

Another evening he saw her and again she smiled and ran into the forest. This time he asked his fellow officers to look for her, but their search was to no avail. After many days he found her near the present site of Robertson's Folly. As he approached her, she backed closer and closer to the edge of the cliff. He knew she couldn't evade him this time and that he would learn her identity. He went nearer and she backed so close to the edge that he feared for her safety. As he reached to save her, she threw herself backwards over the cliff drawing him with her. The next morning only Captain Robertson's body was found on the rocks below. There was no sign of the Indian maiden.

Indian legends form a background for the recorded history of Mackinac Island and represent here the Island of Mackinac before the white man.

This Fort Mackinac Guard House and cannon overlook Mackinac Harbor.

Mackinac Island about 1880.

MACKINAC ISLAND

AS HISTORY RECORDS IT

Michilimackinac, the original name for the area of the Straits region, included the present locations of Mackinaw City and St. Ignace as well as Mackinac Island, and was the home of the Algonquin and Huron Indians. The Ottawas or the Chippewas were members of the Algonquin tribe and lived in peace in the area of the Straits of Michilimackinac until the Iroquois were driven from the east into the area.

Champlain was the first white man to contact the Ottawa nation. He found numbers of Ottawas in 1615 near the mouth of the French river in Georgian Bay. Nineteen years later members of this tribe were at Michilimackinac.

Champlain was a member of a company, One Hundred Associates Company, which was chartered by Louis the XIII, King of France, and granted forever Quebec, all New France, which included Michilimackinac, and territory as far south as Florida. In 1627 The King gave the company almost sovereign power with the stipulation that only the Roman Catholic Church be established.

Two years later the British captured all this territory but the whole country was returned by treaty in 1632. In 1633 Champlain was again in command of Quebec and New France. It was at this time that Jean Nicolet was instructed by Champlain to travel with a group of Hurons, who had come to Quebec to trade. He was to go to Green Bay, Wisconsin, the southern extent of New France, and make a treaty with the Indians there.

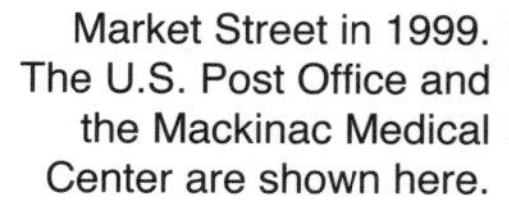

Market Street in 1999. The U.S. Post Office and the Mackinac Medical Center are shown here.

1634 Jean Nicolet, made this voyage and was the first white man to visit Michilimackinac. In his honor a bronze tablet was unveiled in 1915 at **Nicolet Watch Tower** under the auspices of the Michigan Historical Society, the Mackinac Island State Park Commission and the City of Mackinac Island. The watch tower, overlooking Arch Rock, might well have given Nicolet an excellent view of the Straits of Mackinac and the Les Cheneaux Islands. In compliance with Champlain's instructions, Jean Nicolet traveled with the Hurons, taking the Ottawa route, Lake Nipissing, and Georgian Bay, toward the land of the Winnebagoes.

Nicolet's arrival in 1634.

Nicolet was convoyed by seven friendly Indians in birch bark canoes. Passing westward by the mouth of the French river, he found on the main land the "Nation of Beavers," an Indian tribe named for their principal divinity. These natives, whose original home was the Beaver Islands in Lake Huron, were named by the French Nez Perces, owing to their habit of wearing ornaments and feathers thrust through their noses.

Nicolet's Indians pressed onward, entered the St. Mary's river at DeTour and paddled up the stream of the falls. The Indians they encountered at the Sault were Algonquins and Ojibways or Chippewas. After a short stay at Sault Ste. Marie, Nicolet returned down the river in his canoes, propelled by the seven Hurons. On reaching the mouth of the river they made the turn at DeTour and going along the shore of the upper peninsula they passed Les Cheneaux (the channels), St. Martin's Islands, St. Ignace, the Island of Michilimackinac, Gros Cap and Seul Choix in succession, until they turned from Lake Michigan into Bay de Noquet. Here Nicolet visited a tribe called Roqui and Noquet, or bear family, Algonquins classed with Chippewas. Farther up the river he came to the Menominees on a river of the same name.

They were Algonquins of a lighter color, and their language was not easy to understand. After a short stay here he resumed his voyage to the Winnebagoes, to whom he sent one of the Hurons in advance. The Indian, who was well received, foretold his coming and his message of peace. The Winnebagoes sent several of their young men to meet him. Arriving, he advanced, clothed in a robe of "Chinese damask sprinkled with flowers of different colors," and carrying a pistol in each hand, both of which he discharged in the air to the right and left. The women and children flew in dismay, for he was a "Manitou," who carried thunder in his hands. The Winnebagoes were found to be numerous. Their language was different from any Algonquins or Hurons, since they were Dakota stock. At that time the Sacs and Foxes had not arrived: they came at a later period.

Hearing from his scout of Nicolet's coming, four or five thousand natives of the different tribes assembled to meet him in council. Nicolet made an alliance with them and urged them to keep the peace with each other and the tribes eastward of Lake Huron and with the Hurons and Nez Perces.

After the treaty he visited the Mascoutins, six days' journey up the Fox river. From this tribe Nicolet got confused stories of the Mississippi, which were so mixed with the Wisconsin that he could not get a definite idea of what he and others supposed was the "sea", distant only three days journey. From here he went southward and visited the Illinois tribe on the prairies and returned to the Winnebagoes. On his return trip he tarried with the Pottawattomies who lived on the island at the mouth of Green Bay.

1635 Nicolet, in this year, after the ice had broken up, traveled by way of the Straits of Michilimackinac and the island of the same name to the south shore of Great Manitoulin Island, where a band of Ottawas lived. The same seven Hurons were with him as his convoy. From that island they crossed Georgian Bay to the Huron villages. That summer he accompanied the Indians on their annual trading trip to a post on the St. Lawrence river. They probably reached Three Rivers about the middle of July in 1635.

1635 Champlain died in the fort of Quebec, December 25. Father Isaac Jogues and Raymbault planted a cross at Sault Ste. Marie, Michigan in 1643. Jean Nicolet was drowned, when a boat upset, on the river of Quebec in October 1642.

1654 Two French Traders, Pierre Esperit Radisson and Medard Chouart des Grocelliers passed by way of Michilimackinac and Point Iroquois (Now St. Ignace) in 1654 on the way to Green Bay. They returned in 1656 with sixty canoes, loaded with furs, and a large party of Hurons and Ottawas, bound for the market at Three Rivers on the St. Lawrence.

About the same time Nicholas Perot made a canoe trip through the Straits of Michilimackinac to Green Bay.

Father Claude Jean Allouez was the first Jesuit missionary known to have visited the Straits of Mackinac. He came from his mission on Chequamegon Bay on Lake Superior.

1668 By this time the French were continually advancing into this part of the continent, while the English, Dutch, Spanish and Portuguese were also advancing their interests. About this time New France was divided into these provinces:

HUDSON BAY, all territory north of latitude 49° and west indefinitely;

QUEBEC, with Canada east, southward to the head of Lake Champlain, and westward to the head waters of the Ohio;

MICHILIMACKINAC, the country west of Quebec, south to and along the Ohio to the western boundary of what is now Minnesota, north to 49' and all the country drained into Lake Superior and Huron.

Michilimackinac was not only the name of the Island of Mackinac but also of a large area of territory surrounding it.

The Province of Detroit was set off from the Michilimackinac territory in 1700. It included all of Canada west above the Cataract of Niagara and north to Lake Huron, that part of Michigan south of Saginaw Bay and most of Ohio and Indiana. The capitol of the Province of Michilimackinac was Mackinac Island. It was not only the seat of justice and base of supplies but the center of trade of a vast territory. It was the headquarters of French traders and trappers and their white and Indian employees.

1671 **Father Jacques Marquette** founded the first mission on the Straits of Mackinac, at Michilimackinac (St. Ignace) in 1671. He came to Mackinac Island in the spring of that year from the mission at La Pointe on Lake Superior, where he had succeeded Father Allouez in 1665. The mission there was broken up when the Hurons and Ottawas abandoned the place in face of a threatening invasion by the Sioux.

Death of Pere Marquette in 1675.

The Hurons went to Mackinac Island, and Father Marquette followed them. Afterwards, finding that Father Dablon had been there the preceding winter, Marquette soon changed to Point St. Ignace and established a mission for the Hurons and Ottawas.

On May 17, 1673, Father Marquette and Louis Joliet, whom he had met in 1671 at the great ceremony of St. Lusson's at the Sault, left Michilimackinac on their great voyage of discovery, reaching the "Father of Waters" at the mouth of the Wisconsin River on the seventeenth of June. They later paddled their birch bark canoes as far south as a point near the mouth of the Arkansas river. Satisfied that the Mississippi emptied, not into the South Sea but into the Gulf of Mexico, Joliet returned to Quebec. Marquette, however, made another voyage down the Mississippi the following year. It was this exploration that hastened his death. He died May 18, 1675 at the age of 38, while returning to St. Ignace from his second journey of exploration. He was attended only by two Indians, who buried him on the banks of a stream, thought by some to have been St. Joseph's River, and by others the Sable River near the present city of Ludington. In 1677, the Kiskakon Indians, whom he had instructed at La Pointe, bore his remains to the Mission chapel at the Straits, where he was buried by Fathers Pierson and Nouvel. The convoy consisted of nearly thirty canoes, including even a goodly number of Iroquois (the Iroquois were the enemies of the Hurons and allied tribes) who had joined the Algonquins to honor the ceremony. As they approached the church, the priest chanted the De Profundis in the presence of all the people and the body remained in state at the little church all that day, Pentecost Monday, June 8, 1677. The next day it was buried with honors under the church. Father Marquette was called "The Guardian Angel of the Ottawa Mission." The mission of St. Ignace was abandoned in 1705, the priests first burning the church to prevent its desecration; and from that time until 1878 Marquette's grave remained in obscurity, notwithstanding repeated efforts to discover it.

Marquette Park, in the foreground, is a garden for the military at Fort Mackinac in this early photo of the village of Mackinac.

A tradition existed among the Indians that the site of the old church was on the shore of the bay. It was through the instrumentality of the Very Reverend Edward Jacker, V.G., in 1878, who was then pastor at St. Ignace, that the remains were found on May 4th of that year by some men clearing ground on the Patrick Murray homestead in St. Ignace where today stands a monument erected by the residents of that town in 1882. About a fourth of the relics found are still preserved in the church at St. Ignace; the remainder are at Marquette University in Milwaukee.

Marquette Statue in Marquette Park below Fort Mackinac on the Island was dedicated on September 1, 1909 in his memory with appropriate ceremonies including an address by the late Justice William R. Day of the Supreme Court of the United States.

1679 LaSalle was in command of Fort Frontenac, Canada when he heard of the discoveries of Marquette and Joliet. He obtained a concession from Count Frontenac, and another from the French King, which allowed him, in the territory which he discovered, the exclusive trade of buffalo and all other articles excepting the fur trade of the Lakes. Courcelle, Governor of Quebec, sent the young adventurer, with a party of priests and wood-rangers southward into the great forests of what is now Ohio. His goal was to find the legendary Father of Waters and to eradicate Spain's faint claim to it.

LaSalle sailed from Fort Frontenac in the **"Griffin,"** the first sailing vessel on the Great Lakes. It was a vessel of about sixty tons, built on his orders just above Niagara Falls and launched on August 7, 1679. The ship reached Mackinac late on August 27 of that year and the men were received with great ceremonies by the chiefs of the Ottawas.

On September 2 the Griffin left Michilimackinac for Green Bay, where it took on a cargo of furs and sailed away into the waters of the Great Lakes and was never heard from again.

1681 LaSalle again visited the Straits of Mackinac on his second voyage to the Mississippi. He reached the mouth of the "Father of Waters" the following year, on the ninth of April and named the country Louisiana, after Louis XIV of France. In 1688 survivors of his fatal expedition from France, in which he aimed to reach the mouth of the great river by water, arrived at Michilimackinac with a tale of disaster.

1688 Baron LaHontan, because of his knowledge of the Indian language and his skill in forest diplomacy, was sent as a commander of troops to the Great Lakes region, in company with Duluth, and built Fort St. Joseph at the foot of Lake Huron, near the present site of Port Huron. Here La Durantaye, commandant at Michilimackinac, sweeping down in 1687 with birch bark canoe loads of Mackinac Indians, took possession of the whole country for France. It was from this post that LaHonton went to Mackinac in 1688 "to buy up corn for the Hurons and Ottawas," as he writes.

1695 M. de Cadillac, who founded Detroit, commanded at Fort St Joseph. He thus describes the place: "It is very important that you know, in case you are not already informed, that this village is one of the largest in Canada. There is a fine fort of pickets, and sixty houses that form a street in a straight line. There is a garrison of well disciplined, chosen soldiers, consisting of about two hundred men, the best formed and most able to be found in this New World; besides many other persons who are residents here during two or three months of the year. The houses are arranged along the shore of this great Lake Huron, and fish and smoked meat constitute the principal food of the inhabitants The villages of the savages, in which are six or seven thousand souls, are about a pistol shot distance from ours. All the lands are clear for about three leagues around the village, and perfectly well cultivated. They produce a sufficient quantity of Indian corn for the use of both French and savage inhabitants."

1701 Cadillac, a few years later, perceived the importance of a fort on the de Troit and went to France to present the subject to Count Ponchartrain the Colonial Minister who accepted the idea favorably. This meant that the area around Michilimackinac was forsaken by the French.

A dispute arose between Cadillac and the Jesuits. The former insisted upon a concentration of French interests in the west, while at Detroit the latter were urging the French Government to re-establish Michilimackinac.

The Jesuits did all in their power to prevent the Indians from removing to Detroit, while Cadillac held out inducements to prevail upon them to desert their village and settle in the vicinity of the new fort, and succeeded so that in 1705, the Jesuits became discouraged, burned their church, and returned to Quebec. But alarmed at this step, the Governor soon prevailed upon Father Marest to return; and shortly after, the Ottawas, who were becoming dissatisfied at Detroit, began to move back to Michilimackinac.

1714 Father Marest now did all in his power to prevail upon the French Government to send M. Louvigay, a former commander, with a few soldiers to re-establish the fort at St. Ignace. He did not succeed until 1714 when the long wished-for garrison and commander arrived, giving new life to the settlement.

1721 Father Charlevoix was at Michilimackinac and wrote as follows: "I arrived the twenty-eighth at this spot, which is much declined since M. de Cadillac drew to Detroit the greater part of the savages who were settled here, and especially the Hurons. Several Ottawas have followed them; others have dispersed themselves in the Beaver Islands. There is only here a middling village where there is still a great trade for peltry, because it is the passage for, or the rendezvous, of many of the savage nations. The fort is preserved and the house of the missionaries, who are not much employed at present, having never found much docility among the Ottawas, but the court thinks their presence necessary in a place where one must often treat with our allies to exercise their ministry among the French who come hither in great numbers. I have been assured that since the settlement at Detroit and the dispersion of the savages occasioned thereby, many nations of the North who used to bring their peltries hither, have taken the route to Hudson Bay. The situation at Michilimackinac is very advantageous for trade. The post is between three great lakes; Lake Michigan, which is three hundred leagues in compass without mentioning the great bay that comes into it: Lake Huron, which is three hundred and fifty leagues in circumference, and which is triangular, and the Upper Lake, which is five hundred leagues."

Charlevoix at the time of this visit in 1721, apparently describes the post and settlement of North Michilimackinac (St. Ignace,) as he says "The fort is preserved, and the house of the missionaries," but does not allude to the church, as that burned in 1705. The movement to South Michilimackinac must have been gradual up to 1760, when the Province of Michilimackinac was transferred to the British.

From the early part until about the middle of the eighteenth century there is little history recorded of the province of Michilimackinac and of the region about the straits of the same name. The establishment of the Province of Detroit and the withdrawal of the troops to the town of Detroit on that strait where many Indians followed, caused a diversion of trade and consequently, a decline of supremacy.

1759 With the victory of the English on the Plains of Abraham, before Quebec, September 12th and 13th,1759, the victorious General Wolf fell, and the defeated General Montcalm was also killed. The subsequent surrender of Montreal and Canada with all its dependencies on the 8th day of September,1760, by the Marquis de Vaudreuil to the British Crown was the opening wedge to a change in history. The Province of Michilimackinac was transferred to Britain, and the French inhabitants remained and the effects of their civil institutions and religion are evident to this day.

The change from French to English rule was not agreeable to the Indians of the Lakes. They liked better the French dominion and their personal relations with the French people than they did the English ways and English associations, and they did not take kindly to the transfer. One reason for this preference is said to have been that the French people were accustomed to pay respects to all the Indians religious or superstitious observances, whereas an Englishman or an American was apt either to take no pains to conceal his contempt for their superstition or to speak out bluntly against them.

1763 This feeling of discontent under the change of empire on the part of the Indians, was fanned and skillfully directed by the great leader and diplomat Pontiac. "The Conspiracy of Pontiac" is the well known title of one of Parman's series of North American history. This conspiracy was no less than a deep and comprehensive scheme, matured by this most crafty savage chief, for a general uprising, in which all English forts, from the south to the upper lakes, were to be attacked simultaneously, and the English rule forever destroyed. The Indians would hauntingly say, "You have conquered the French, but you have not conquered us." Out of twelve forts, nine were taken but not long held.

While this scheme was a failure in its larger aspect, the plot against the old post of Michilimackinac across the water succeeded only too well.

This is a view of Sugar Loaf looking east from Point Lookout.

MASSACRE AT OLD FORT MICHILIMACKINAC

1763 A band of thirty-five English soldiers and their officers formed its garrison. Encamped in the woods not far off was a large number of Indians. One morning in June with a show of friendliness, the Indians invited the soldiers to witness their game of ball just outside the stockade. The Chippewas were to play the Sacs. As this was the birthday of the King of England, the men were in a celebrating mood and some indulgence was shown. Discipline for a time relaxed. Gates were left ajar and the soldiers and officers carelessly sauntered out and looked on, enjoying the sport. In the course of the play, and as part of the prearranged stratagem, the ball was so struck that it fell within the stockade line of the fort. As if pursuing it, the players came rushing to the gate. The soldiers, intent on watching the play, suspected nothing. The Indians now had an open way within, and instantly turned from ball-players into warriors, and a terrifying "whoop" was given. The squaws, sharing in the plot, were standing nearby with tomahawks concealed under their blankets. The surprise of the fort and the success of the Indians were complete.

The details of this event are told by the English trader, **Alexander Henry**, at the time within the stockade, and unfortunately a sharer in the experiences. Excepting the meager report of the capture made by Captain Etherington, the officer in command, there seems to be nothing but the narrative of this English trader. When the fort was captured by the savages, he himself was hidden for the first night, out of their murderous reach. He was discovered the next day. Then followed a series of experiences, escapes and turns of fortune, while all the time the most barbarous fate seemed impending. It was not enough that his goods were confiscated and his clothes stripped off his body, but the savages thirsted for his blood. They said of him and their other prisoners that they were being reserved to "make English broth." After four days of such horror there came a time which Henry says gave "a new color to my lot." During his residence at the post before the massacre, a certain Chippewa Indian named Wawatam, who used to come frequently to his house, had become friendly and told him that the Great Spirit pointed him out as one to adopt as a brother. Suddenly, on the fourth day of his captivity, Wawatam appeared on the scene. Before a council of chiefs he asked the release of his brother the trader. At the same time, he laid down presents to buy off whatever claims any might have thought they had on the prisoner. Wawatam's request, or demand, was granted, and taking Mr. Henry by the hand he led him to his own lodge, where he received the utmost kindness.

A day or two afterwards, fearing an attack of retaliation by the English, the whole body of Indians moved from the fort over to the Island as a place of safety. They landed, three hundred and fifty fighting men, Wawatam was among them, with Henry in safe keeping. Several days passed, then two large canoes from Montreal with English goods aboard were seized by the Indians. The invoice of goods contained among other things a quantity of liquor and soon mad drunkenness prevailed. The watchful and faithful Wawatam told Henry he feared he could not protect him when the Indians were in liquor, and besides, as he frankly confessed, "he could not himself resist the temptation of joining his comrades in the debauch." He therefore took him up the hill and back in the woods and hid him in a cave where he was to remain hidden "until the liquor should be drunk." After an uncomfortable night. Henry discovered next morning to his horror, that he had been lying on a heap of human bones and skulls. This retreat of Henry's is known today as **Skull Cave**. It is located not far from Fort Mackinac.

1765 Major Robert Rogers, made famous by Kenneth Robert's "NORTHWEST PASSAGE," took command of the Fort at Old Mackinac which post he held until 1768 when he was accused of conspiring to sack the fort and deliver the post over to the Spanish.

1779 On the 4th of October, Major Patrick Sinclair, Lieutenant-Governor, arrived and assumed command of Michilimackinac relieving Major DePeyster, who left for Detroit on October 15th.

The English previously had secured from the Chippewa Chief a title to Mackinac Island with the idea of removing the fort from Old Mackinac, now Mackinaw City, to Mackinac Island as a safety measure against the Americans.

To achieve this, Major Sinclair sent to the Island on November 6, the sloop of war, **Welcome,** with workmen and the timbers of a house to be erected for them. The government house was erected below the present fort. In February and March, 1780, when the ice was firm, the Catholic Church on the south shore was taken down, the logs hauled over, and the church rebuilt on the old cemetery lot. A government wharf was built of log cribs filled with stone in the bay in front of the present south sally port. On the 4th of November that same year Lieutenant-Governor Sinclair moved over to the Island and established his headquarters. During the winter a blockhouse was completed east of the government house and the present Indian Dormitory.

During the fall of 1780 the sash, doors, casings and other woodwork of many buildings were sent over in vessels to the Island, and in the following winter the logs and timbers were hauled over on the ice. When spring came, the traders pulled down their buildings and rafted them to the Island, where the logs were again put up. Their provisions and goods were sent in boats. The entire movement of the troops was not completed until late in the summer of 1781. The British continued to improve the fort and strengthen the position until 1796, when their troops were withdrawn to St. Joseph's Island.

1783 At the close of 1783 the independence of the United States of America was acknowledged by Great Britain and by the terms of the Treaty of Paris September 3, 1783. The post of Michilimackinac Island with others on the lakes became part of the Republic. On various pretexts the British retained possession of this and other forts until after the treaty promulgated on the 29th of February, 1796, in which it was stipulated that the British troops should be withdrawn from posts within the boundaries by June 1, 1796.

1796 The First United States troops to occupy **Fort Mackinac** Island were in command of Major Henry Burdeck, who, with one company of Artillerists and Engineers, and a company of the 1st Infantry and three officers arrived in October, 1796 and took possession. The British retired to the island of St. Joseph, on the Canadian side a little above DeTour, and established a fort there.

Fort Mackinac is located 133 feet above the Straits of Mackinac and commands the town and harbor of Mackinac. The original stone walls and blockhouses of the Fort still stand and are one of the picturesque features of the Island.

1802 Rev. David Bacon came here as the first Protestant to preach on the Island. He was a representative of the Connecticut Missionary Society.

1808 John Jacob Astor founded the **American Fur Company** in New York in 1808. Later, foreseeing a great future in the Great Lakes region, he sent his agents westward to locate a trading post, and they chose Mackinac Island. A fur warehouse was built about 1810. Other buildings were added in 1817 including an agency home **(Stuart House)** and clerk's quarters. The Agent's house was a three-story building. The store included a low-ceilinged room with hand hewn beams, and was attached to the two and a half story warehouses where furs were stored. A third unit housed the employees. At the height of its success the **American Fur Company** and its subsidiaries employed four hundred clerks at Mackinac Island as well as two thousand trappers and voyagers. Furs valued at $3,000,000 were handled annually. In 1834, Astor transferred his stock charter to Ramsey Crooks & Associates, who continued as usual until 1842, when because of competition and other causes the company's career ended on Mackinac Island.

1812 On July 27th of this year the British captured Fort Mackinac. The British landed at the back of the Island at a point now called **British Landing** and dragged their cannon to Fort George, now called **Fort Holmes**, where they commanded Fort Mackinac below them. This was one of the first actions of the war. Lieutenant Hanks commanded Fort Mackinac and the position in which he found himself on the morning of the surrender made him a victim of circumstances beyond his control. The British at both Detroit and St. Joseph's Island had news of the declaration of war. However, the news was not received at Mackinac. Captain Roberts at St. Joseph acted immediately. All the available fur-traders and Indians were quickly added to his troops at St. Joseph. The first intimation of trouble the Americans at Mackinac had was the movement of the Indians. Michael Dousman, who set out to see what it was all about was made a prisoner and was informed that any resistance on the part of the Americans would result in the massacre of all regardless of age or sex. He was allowed to mass the citizens at the Old Distillery under a British guard. Small wonder they should urge him and other influential citizens to counsel Hank to surrender unconditionally. Reinforcing this appeal to humanity was that of the menacing guns on the heights above Fort Mackinac, which the British had placed there in the night. (Later, Lieutenant Hanks was killed by a cannon shot at the bombardment of Detroit.) After the surrender, the citizens were assembled at the government house to take the oath of allegiance to the British Crown. Most of them willingly did this. The British troops held the fort and Island until the summer of 1815 after the close of the war.

Although the British had captured the Island without bloodshed, they were in constant fear of attack from the land and naval forces of the United States. After the memorable naval battle near the head of Lake Erie between Perry and Barclay September 10, 1813, when the entire British fleet of six vessels was captured or destroyed, the tide had turned and the chances of invasion were imminent.

1814

In April an expedition was proposed to capture Mackinac Island. Orders were issued June 2, and a fleet of vessels fitted out, with Commodore Sinclair on board with a landing force of seven hundred and fifty officers and men, Lieutenant-Colonel Croghan commanding. They sailed July 3, but bad weather and uncharted routes without a pilot delayed them so that they did not reach the vicinity of the Island until the latter part of the month. After hovering about for a week it was concluded there was no better plan than to copy the previously successful plot of the British and land on the north end of the Island at **"British Landing".** They were ambushed on the **Battle Field**, the site of the Early farm, and forced to retreat to their boats. This was done and the expedition left the Island with fifteen killed and about fifty wounded. Major Andrew Hunter Holmes, next in command to Colonel Croghan was one of the slain in this unfortunate action. He fell while leading his battalion in a flanking movement on the right. A Spaniard and a Winnebago chief, Yellow Dog, both claimed that they killed the Major. The body of Major Holmes was recovered after the battle and taken to Detroit for internment.

The heights above Fort Mackinac had been named Fort George by the British when they fortified them after the capture of Mackinac. However, this point, 325 feet above the Straits was renamed Fort Holmes, in honor of Major Holmes. It was destroyed by the Americans after the war.

Major Andrew Hunter Holmes was killed in the Battle of Mackinac Island, August 4, 1814, in an attempt to take the fort from the British. When the American forces took possession of the Island after the war the name was changed from Fort George to Fort Holmes in honor of the major who fell in battle.

1814 The Americans' ambition to regain the Island was not abandoned with the defeat at the Battle of Mackinac in 1814. They tried to starve the garrison out and thus force a surrender. Two vessels, The "Tigress" and the "Scorpion," were detached from the fleet and left to maintain a strict blockade. This proved effective, and provisions ran so low in Mackinac that a loaf of bread sold for one dollar and the men of the garrison were killing horses for meat.

But relief, and that by their own daring, was at hand for the besieged garrison. Lieutenant Worsely, with seventeen sailors of the Royal Navy, had managed to escape when the American fleet destroyed the "Nancy" and the block house of Nottawasaga and had made passage in an open boat to the Fort at Mackinac. Forced by the necessity of the situation, the capture of the two blockading vessels was planned. Batteaux trading canoes were manned under Lieutenant Worsley with his seamen and volunteers from the garrison, making in all about seventy men. On a dark night, rowing rapidly and silently, they approached first the "Tigress", and taking it completely by surprise, leaped aboard and after a hand to hand struggle soon had possession. Two days later the "Scorpion" was sighted coming toward her companion ship, unaware of its change in fortune. Since night was coming on, she anchored some two miles off. About daylight the Tigress set sail, swept down on the Scorpion, opened fire, boarded and captured her. That was the final stroke to the ill fated expedition and Mackinac was secure for another winter.

1814 The defeat of August 4, with the subsequent connected events, was a disastrous defeat to the United States. Had it not been for the terms of the treaty of peace, ratified the following year, the continued occupation of the Fort and the Straits by the British would have been of far-reaching effect on the commercial industrial interest of the nation.

Alexis St. Martin is shown being examined by Dr. William S. Beaumont after he had been shot in the stomach

Peace was concluded between the two contending nations during the winter of 1814–15, as a result of the Treaty of Ghent, December 24, 1814.

1815 The American spirit and regime were soon fully restored after the repossession by our troops in 1815. From that time on there was a long succession of regular army soldiers and officers inhabiting the old quarters and barracks. Many of the officers who afterwards acquired high rank and distinction during the Civil War, 1861–1865, either in the Union or Southern Army, had been in service on the Island as young Captains or Lieutenants. General Pemberton once served here and 23 years later was a General and commander at Vicksburg with Grant's besieging armies around him.

1817 Mackinac was incorporated as a village.

1819 **Walk In The Water,** the first steamboat on the Great Lakes visited Mackinac Island.

1820 Henry R Schoolcraft, world wide authority on the Northern Indians, visited Mackinac Island with an official expedition led by Michigan Territorial Governor Lewis Cass.

1821 Alexis St. Martin, a nineteen-year old French Canadian, was accidently shot in a retail store of the American Fur Company. The Fort Surgeon Dr. William S. Beaumont, reached the scene within minutes and treated St. Martin for a wound directly into his stomach. Although he was expected to die immediately, he lived and gave Dr. Beaumont the opportunity to begin his internationally famous experiments on digestion. The experiments which led to the knowledge of digestion as it is now known were carried out through the wound which never healed.

Mackinac's oldest house. The Biddle House, before it was restored. It is now part of the Mackinac Historic Parks exhibits.

The Beaumont building, a former retail store was restored by contributions of the Doctors of Michigan and after its dedication on July 17, 1954 stands as a memorial to Dr. Beaumont.

The only eye witness who left a written account of this shooting was Gurdon Hubbard, who was at that time an employee of the **American Fur Company** and later one of five charter signers of the City of Chicago.

A granite monument to Dr. William Beaumont stands at Fort Mackinac next to the Officers Quarters. It was unveiled in 1900 by the Upper Peninsula and State Medical Societies.

1823 The first Presbyterian Mission on Mackinac Island was established under the auspices of the United Missionary Society by the Reverend William Montague Ferry. The **Mission House**, located on the east boulevard, was built two years later, and in 1830, as the school became stronger, the **Old Mission Church** was erected. During the year of occupation as many as 200 students were in attendance at the school at one time.

A son of Rev Ferry, Thomas White Ferry, was born in the mission during this period and was later United States Senator from Michigan.

Ed Franks and his wife opened the **Mission House** and operated it as a hotel for over 100 years. It was in room 16 that Edward Everett Hale wrote the immortal **"Man Without A Country"** while waiting for a boat bound for Lake Superior. Among noted guests to visit Mission House have been Generals Sheridan, Sherman and Hancock.

The history of the **Old Mission Church** is closely linked with that of the Mission House. The school attracted scholars from all the surrounding country. Church and school grew with the prosperity and importance of Mackinac, flourished for a few years and then declined with the shrinking of the Island's population, until in 1837, after having enrolled some 500 scholars, the mission was abandoned, and the church was closed. For a time it was practically unused until in 1895 it was reopened as the Union Chapel of Mackinac Island. Its original style has been preserved including the straight-backed pews with doors, old time pulpit, high choir gallery, and small–paned windows. It is now part of the Mackinac Island State Park.

The Old Mission Church is now part of Mackinac Historic Parks and is sometimes used for weddings.

1833-41 Henry R. Schoolcraft was sent to Mackinac Island as Indian Agent by the U.S. Government. He was accompanied by his wife, Jane Johnston Schoolcraft, daughter of the Irish trader, John Johnston and his Indian wife, of a famed Sault family.

1834 John Jacob Astor retired from the **American Fur Company** and was succeeded by Ramsey Crooks as president.

1836 Mackinac was beginning to be known as a summer resort about this time. Among visitors from England in this year was Miss Harriet Martineau of English literary fame. She spent two years in this country traveling and writing of her experiences. She described Mackinac in this way. "We saw a white speck before us. It was the barracks of Mackinac stretching along the side of the green hills and clearly visible before the town came into view. The Island looked enchanting as we approached, as I think it always must, though we had the advantage of seeing it first in the most golden sunshine that ever hallowed lake or shore. The colors were upon all the little vessels in the harbor. The national flag streamed from the garrison. The soldiers thronged the walls of the barracks: half-breed boys were paddling about in their canoes, in the transparent waters: the half French, half Indian population of the place were all abroad in their best. An Indian lodge was on the shore and a picturesque dark group stood beside it. The cows were coming down the steep slope to the milking. Nothing could be more bright and joyous."

The Mission House was built as a dormitory for the Mission School.

She tells of a walk on the Island. "No words can give an idea of the charms of this morning walk. We wound about in a vast shrubbery with ripe strawberries under foot, wild flowers all around, and scattered knolls; and opening vistas tempting curiosity in every direction." Especially charming and impressive, she thought, was the vista from Fort Holmes. As she looked out on the glassy lake and the green tufted islands, she compared it to what Noah might have seen the first bright morning after the deluge. "Such a cluster of little paradises rising out of such a congregation of waters. Blue waters in every direction, wholly unlike any aspect of the sea: cloud shadows and specks of white vessels. Bowery islands rise out of it, bowery promontories stretch down into it; while at ones feet lies the melting beauty which one almost fears will vanish in its softness before one's eyes; the beauty of the shadowy dells and sunny mounds, with browsing cattle and springing fruit and flowers. Thus would I fain think, did the world emerg from the flood."

In reference to her departure she writes: "We were in great delight at having seen Mackinac, at having the possession of its singular imagery life. But this delight was dashed with the sorrow of leaving it. I could not have believed how deeply it is possible to regret a place, after so brief an acquaintance with it." And here is Miss Martineau's final tribute of admiration: "From place to place in my previous traveling, I have been told of the charms of the lakes, and especially of the Island of Mackinac. The Island is chiefly known as a principal station of the Northwestern Fur Company. Others know it as the seat of an Indian Mission. Others again, as a frontier garrison. It is known to me as the wildest and tenderest piece of beauty that I have yet seen on God's earth."

1837 A visitor this year was Captain Marryatt, first an officer of celebrity in the English navy, but better known in this country as a novelist of sea tales, was here during the summer. In his "Diary of America" he writes of Mackinac. "It has the appearance of a fairy island floating on the water, which is so pure and transparent that you may see down to almost any depth, and the air above is as pure as the water, that you feel invigorated as you breath it. The first reminiscence brought to my mind after I had landed was the description by Walter Scott of the island residence of Magnus Trail and his daughters Minna and Brenda in the novel, "The Pirate." The appearance of the village streets, largely given to sails, cordage, nets, fish barrels, and the like, still further suggested the resemblance in his mind, and he says he might have imagined himself "transferred to the Shetland Isle. had it not been for the lodges of the Indians on the beach, and the Indians themselves, either running about or lying on the porches before the whisky stores."

1837 Michigan became a State with Lewis Cass as the First Governor.

1841 Prince De Joinville, son of Louis Philippe, King of France, visited Mackinac.

1843 Countess Ossoli, better known in this country as Margaret Fuller of Boston, spent nine days in Mackinac as part of a journey she made in the northwest and which she described in her book, "Summer On The Lakes." She arrived at a time when several thousand Indians were encamped on the beach to receive their annual payments from the government. As the vessel came into the harbor "The Captain had some rockets set off which greatly excited the Indians, and their wild cries resounded along the shores." The Island was " a scene of loveliness, and the wild forms adorned it as looking so at home in it," She represents it as a "pleasing sight after the raw, crude, staring assemblage of houses everywhere sure to be met in this country, to see the French town, mellow in its coloring, and with the harmonious effect of a slow growth which assimilates naturally with objects around it." Concerning Arch Rock, she says "The arch is perfect whether you look up through it from the lake, or down through it to the transparent water." She both ascended and descended "the steep and crumbling path, and rested at the summit beneath the trees, and at the foot upon the cool and mossy stones beside the lapping waves."

The cannon in Fort Mackinac command the Straits of Mackinac.

The woods she described as "very full in foliage, and in August showed tender green and pliant life of June elsewhere." She gives us a view from the bluff on the harbor side: "I never wished to see a more fascinating picture. It was an hour of the deepest serenity: bright blue and gold with rich shadows. Every moment the sunlight felt more mellow. The Indians were grouped and scattered among the lodges: the women preparing food over the many small fires: the children, half naked, wild as little goblins, were playing both in and out of the water; bark canoes upturned upon the beach, and others coming, their square sails set and with almost arrowy speed." And a familiar picture is this: "Those evenings were very happy, looking over the old-fashioned garden, over the beach, and the pretty island opposite, beneath the glowing moon."

1846 William Cullen Bryant visited Mackinac and describes his trip in his book "Letters to a Traveler."

1850 James Jesse Strang was crowned "King" at his Mormon capitol city, St. James, on nearby Beaver Island. Later his murderer was imprisoned for trial at the Mackinac County Court House on the site of the present City Hall.

1854-1860 The fishing industry grew in importance and replaced the fur trade in primary importance on Mackinac Island. Lake fishing for the commercial trade began about 1824 when small shipments of salted and barreled trout and whitefish were shipped to the Boston markets. This increased until in some years as many as 250,000 barrels of fish per year were shipped from the region of Michilimackinac.

The fish, some weighing as much as 85 pounds, were cleaned and placed in barrels between layers of salt. A part of the industry at Mackinac Island was the construction of the barrels used in shipping the fish, and the men on the Island spent the winter in this occupation. The barrels of fish were shipped via schooner to such places as the Fulton Street Market in New York City and were handled by such large fishing companies as the Booth Fisheries of Saginaw.

Net tending during the summer was usually done with the use of a Mackinac boat, previously used in the fur trade and now adopted to the fishing industry. These boats with two spars, two mainsails and a jib, were loaded with fish which brought only about two and a half cents a pound in the market. A person could meet one of the boats and enjoy the privilege of choosing any fish in the boat for a dime.

The “Mackinac” boat was used for work and pleasure.

From Foley's Art Gallery

Leads and floats in use today were not available at that time and their function was filled by rocks in the case of the leads and by wooden, pine or cedar, floats pointed at one end and notched at the other so that they floated vertically in the water. Fishing was continued during the winter through the ice with the use of nets and also with the aid of jib rigs which caught the trout and kept them alive until the fishermen tended their lines.

A schooner of the type that carried fish from Mackinac. This light house on the point of Round Island, south of Mackinac Island, was abandoned in 1935 by the U.S. Light House Service. The light in the tower was maintained by the U.S. Coast Guard until 1948. The light has recently been replaced and is powered by solar batteries.

The women of the Island spent part of their winter making and repairing the nets for the coming season and in making fish oil which found many uses. One of the these was the polishing of the horses hoofs.

Whitefish and trout were the only marketable fish at this time and sturgeon that were caught were "piled up like cord wood on the beach."

Main street Mackinac Island before the turn of the century.

1855 Longfellow published his well known poem "Hiawatha" for which **Hiawatha Spring**, midway up the bluff by **Dwightwood Spring** on the eastern shore of the Island is named.

1861-1865 During the Civil War, all regular army troops were withdrawn temporarily from Fort Mackinac except for a solitary sergeant. During part of the war Confederate prisoners were housed in the Fort, and in 1862 the Steamer Illinois brought to the Island three distinguished prisoners of war from Tennessee.

At the close of the war, the Fort resumed its old time service as a garrison post with about 50 men, of the regular army, with its officers, composing the force.

1870 "Anne" a novel of Mackinac Island, by Constance Fenimore Woolson, who had visited Mackinac in 1870, was published. Her brother was novelist James Fenimore Cooper. **Anne's Tablet,** commemorating Miss Cooper is located on the bluff just east of Fort Mackinac. It is a beautiful place to visit and has a commanding view of the harbor and city. It was erected in 1916.

1873 Father Moise Mainville began the construction of the present STE. ANNE'S CHURCH which stands on the site of an earlier church, which was moved here between 1825-27.

1825-27 The Catholic Church was located near the present site of the Windsor Hotel from 1780 until 1825. The present church was entirely refurbished in 1996.

1875 Mackinac Island became a National Park under the control of the Commandant at Fort Mackinac. Of the 2200 acres that make up the Island about 81 percent are in the Park.

The Grand Hotel was built in 1887 and has been enlarged a number of times since.

1882 The county seat of Mackinac County was transferred to St. Ignace. The City Hall stands on the site of the original court house.

Trinity Episcopal Church was erected below Fort Mackinac.

1887 **Grand Hotel** opened on July 10th. Senator Francis B. Stockbridge, of Michigan had purchased the site of the Hotel five years earlier and had vowed to hold the property for the construction of the world's largest and finest summer hotel. John Oliver Plank, the outstanding resort hotel operator of the time, became interested in the venture and undertook it. Stockholders in the company included officials of the Detroit & Cleveland Navigation Company, the Pennsylvania Railroad, and the New York Central Railroad. Commodore Cornelius Vanderbilt was the first president of the Company.

The hotel was advertised as "Plank's Grand Hotel" until 1890 when Mr. Plank sold his interest. The original hotel was about one half of its present size. It was enlarged in 1897 and again in 1912 and was entirely remodeled in 1919. The porch floor 100 feet above the lake level is 660 feet in length. Mr. W.S. Woodfill purchased the hotel in 1933. Since that time he and the Musser family, who are the present owners, have continuously upgraded, enlarged and enhanced the facilities.

Some noted guests the first season included Mrs. Potter Palmer, who arrived on opening day with three teams of horses, saddle horses, tally-ho and carriages; members of the Swift, Cudahy, and Armour families of Chicago; General Leonard Wood, who made this his headquarters during the summer of 1920 when he was a presidential candidate; Samuel Clemens (Mark Twain); Marshall Field; Potter Palmer; Cornelius Vanderbilt; George Pullman, and George Eastman.

Fort Mackinac troops parading behind the Fort

Governor Cyrus G. Luce of Michigan spent the entire summer on Mackinac in 1887 and ever since it has been the custom of Michigan Governors to make Mackinac Island their summer headquarters.

1895 After almost continuous military occupation since **1675** (except from 1701-1714 when the French abandoned the area) the United States Government moved its garrison from Mackinac Island to Fort Brady at Sault Ste. Marie.

The National Park at Mackinac Island, including all the lands under control by the Commandant at Fort Mackinac, were turned over to the State of Michigan for use as a State Park under the control of a State Commission.

The first **Mackinac Island State Park Commission** consisted of five members appointed by the Governor John T. Rich, an ex-officio member. They were George T. Arnold, W.M. Clark, Thomas W. Ferry, A.L. Stevens, and Peter White. The first Superintendent of the Park was Homer L. Thayer of Lansing.

Soon after this automobiles were banned within the State Park by the Commission. It was not until May 1, 1930, that an ordinance of the City of Mackinac Island officially banned motor vehicles.

1895 The United States Lighthouse Service built and placed in commission a lighthouse on the point of Round Island, just south of Mackinac Island. This light was tended by keepers living on Round Island with their families. There are no other buildings or inhabitants on Round Island. After 1916 sailors from the Mackinac Island Coast Guard Station operated the light. It was abandoned in 1935 and replaced by the lighthouse in the center of the Straits of Mackinac in 1948.

After the fur trade dwindled, the John Jacob Astor buildings were formed into the Astor hotel seen here in this winter scene of Market Street. The tower of the City Hall is in the background.

Mackinac has been a long time tourist destination and here visitors arrive from two cruise ships. In this era it was possible to purchase steamboat tickets and railroad tickets in the Arnold Line ticket office.

The Little Stone Church, built in 1904 is the site of about 40 weddings each summer.

1898 The Chicago to Mackinac Yacht race began this year when five yachts raced to Mackinac Island from Chicago. A cup was presented to the winner for the first time in 1906. This cup in the shape of an Indian War canoe stands in the Chicago Yacht Club at Belmont Harbor. The Detroit-Mackinac race began much later than this.

1899 Mackinac Island was incorporated as a city.

1904 The **Little Stone Church,** Union Congregational, was built on the boulevard leading to the Grand Hotel. Three of the stained glass windows, a memorial to Gurdon Hubbard, depict Robert Stewart, his clerks, the Rev Ferry, and Shusco, a converted Indian conjurer. The windows were done in New York by contemporaries of Tiffany.

1909 A statue of Father Marquette was formally dedicated in **Marquette Park** on the water front at Mackinac Island. Funds for the statue were obtained from the pennies of Michigan school children.

1915 **Cass Monument,** on the bluff east of Fort Mackinac, was erected on August 28th. It honors General Cass, Governor of Michigan Territory from 1813 to 1831 and is located at **Cass Cliff** above Marquette Park and east of Fort Mackinac.

1916 A United States Coast Guard Station was built east of the Chippewa Hotel in 1916. It was donated to the Mackinac Island State Park in 1970 for a Visitor Center when a new station was built in St. Ignace in 1969. The Coast Guard Cutter "Mackinac" is stationed during parts of the year at Cheboygan, Michigan. It keeps the ice channels open and takes the vessels thru the Straits of Mackinac during the winter season.

A view of Mackinac village and harbor before 1900, taken from Fort Mackinac.

1931 Mackinac Island was cited as **"Michigan's Most Historic Spot"** by the D. A. R. in August when they dedicated a tablet in Marquette Park.

1935 The Mackinac Island State Park Commission first set aside one of the houses within the Fort for the use of the Governor of Michigan. Ten years later the present Governor's summer home was purchased by the State for this purpose. Michigan's Governors had been spending part of their summers at Mackinac for many years before this.

1940 A memorial to former Governor Frank Fitzgerald was erected in the Governor's Garden at Fort Mackinac.

1941 The John Jacob Astor Company buildings were restored to their original form after many years of use as a hotel. This was part of an historical restoration program begun by city and state governments.

The State Park Commission was increased from five to six members, the sixth to be a resident of the Island and to be nominated by the mayor of Mackinac Island.

A festival, "Old Mackinac Lives Again," was performed on Mackinac during August of this year. Katherine Foley, a sister of Mrs. Herbert Benjamin, was chairperson of the event.

1942 MRA came to Mackinac Island when Frank Buchman, an American evangelist leased the Island House hotel. He was head of the Oxford Group and in 1938 had founded Moral Re-Armament.

Thousand foot freighters, like this one, pass through the Straits in the spring while there is still ice.

The group transformed the Island hotel into a training center. In 1950 they purchased property on Mission Point and in the next few years built a number of facilities for training including a conference center

In 1965, Buchman's successor, Peter Howard, was involved in founding Mackinac College, which was able to use the MRA facilities during the winter months. The cold Mackinac winters proved disadvantageous to the growth of the college and it remained open only long enough to graduate its first class. With its close the MRA operations moved to Caux, Switzerland. When the college closed the properties and real estate grew into the present day **Mission Point Resort.**

1945 The National Governors' Conference was held at Mackinac Island with headquarters at the Grand Hotel. Among those present were Governor Harold Stassen, Governor Earl Warren, Governor Thomas Dewey. General George Marshall, and Admiral King.

This view of the Mackinac harbor was taken before 1895. Marquette Park, in the foreground was a garden for the military at the fort.

Governor G. Mennen Williams and Nancy entertained Harry Truman and Vice President Barkley at Mackinac Island.

When Round Island Light was decommissioned in 1947, this lighthouse was built in the middle of the Straits. Besides a light for shipping it had a "pleasant" fog horn, in contrast to the Round Island horn that was deep and penetrating and shook windows as it blew every 30 seconds on foggy mornings. Fort Mackinac and the Governor's summer home are visible on the "Hill of History" as some authors have named it.

1947 **"This Time for Keeps"** starring Esther Williams and Jimmv Durante, a Metro–Goldwyn–Mayer production, was filmed on Mackinac Island.

1948 The Lighthouse in the channel south of Mackinac was commissioned. When built, it was one of the most modern on the Great Lakes. Since it is controlled completely from the shore, no Coast Guardsman is needed at the light. It has its own electric plant so that in case of a power failure locally it would be able to continue without interruption the fog signal, light, and radio signal which it sends out.

1948 **The Mackinac Island Carriage Tour Corporation** was formed. Many of the carriage owners on the Island joined together in order to reduce costs and provide the visitor with better transportation and a more convenient means of sightseeing on the Island.

1950 The **Statue of Liberty** replica on the beach by the Yacht Dock was dedicated May 26, 1950 when the Scenic Trails Council of the Boy Scouts of America dedicated it to the people of Michigan as a gift from the Scouts of this State.

1951 Vice President Barkley visited Mackinac Island to speak before the convention of the Michigan Democratic Party at the Grand Hotel.

1953 The world's largest horse and buggy stable is built on Mackinac Island by Carriage Tour.

1954 On July 17, The Michigan State Medical Society dedicated the **Beaumont Memorial Building** which had been restored by voluntary contributions of Michigan's Doctors and presented to the People of Michigan.

In the years before Mackinac's carriage drivers formed Mackinac Island Carriage Tour Inc., the carriages lined up on Main Street early in the day to be ready for the arrival of the tourists. Now the horses do not need to spend so much time waiting on the street.

1957 The **Mackinac Bridge** was opened to traffic to replace the State owned auto-ferries that carried automobiles across the Straits of Mackinac from Mackinaw City to St, Ignace.

The **Mackinac Island Health Center** was built through the efforts of a local committee.

1958 Fort Mackinac's continuing restoration program was begun.

1959 A new United States Post Office was dedicated. The building is typical of the architecture of the Clerks' Quarters of the Astor Fur Company upon who's site the building stands.

1959 The **Biddle House,** Mackinac's oldest was restored through the efforts of Michigan Architects.

A **Jesuit Chapel** was built as a part of a Fort Mackinac restoration program. It is a historical monument to the early Jesuit Missionaries of the Straits area. Life size figures portray a religious rite of nearly 300 years ago. The Chapel is bark covered in keeping with Indian custom of the area.

Queen Elizabeth II and Prince Phillip of Great Britain passed through the Straits of Mackinac on the yacht Britannia, after the opening ceremonies of the Saint Lawrence Seaway.

1962 A Roman Catholic shrine to Ste. Anne was dedicated next to Ste. Anne's Church.

1965 An enlarged airport facility was dedicated, to be open all year. It made Mackinac more easily accessible in winter and summer.

The Michigan Waterways Commission dedicated an addition to the yacht pier. A number of additions have been added since.

The cruise ships North and South American and the Alabama were weekly visitors to Mackinac Island for many years.

1966 **Indian Agency House** was restored, dedicated and re-opened after having been used as a school for many years.

1970 The **Benjamin Blacksmith Shop,** was restored on Market Street. The building, blacksmith equipment and supplies were provided by the Benjamin family in memory of Herbert Benjamin who had worked on the Island as a blacksmith for more than 60 years.

1971 Rex Humbard, Television Evangelist, bought **Mackinac College** and planned to reopen it. Plans included restoration of the Mission House as an Island Museum and development of a ski center on the Island.

Island House Hotel was restored and reconstructed.

1979 **"Somewhere In Time"** was filmed at Mackinac with Christopher Reeve and Jane Seymour starring. Victorian Mackinac looked great.

1995 **Mackinac Island State Historic Parks** celebrates 100 years as a State Park.

2008 **Mackinac Island Yacht Harbor** is refurbished

2009 The ice breaker *Mackinaw* is retired and is now a museum in Mackinaw City. A NEW *Mackinaw* is dedicated and placed in service.

2011 Mackinac Art Museum opened by the Mackinac State Parks in the Indian Agency House next to Marquette Park.

Mackinac Island with the Upper Peninsula in the background.

TODAY

Mackinac Island is one of Michigan's and America's most famous summer resorts, famous not only for its historic background but for its modern charm and beauty. The Indians called Mackinac Island "the place of the Great Dancing Spirit, the loveliest spot in creation." Men of other races have fallen under Mackinac's magic charm as readily as did the Indian.

Today Mackinac is still free of the noise of the automobile and bus. Vacationists and residents alike call for the horse and buggy of by-gone days when they wish a taxi or a sight seeing ride.

Besides the automobile, Mackinac is well-known for other things that it does not have. Mosquitoes and flies abhor the Island. Since there is no hot weather, nights are cool and sleepable. There is no hayfever.

The vacationists here can find many things to occupy their time. The carriage ride is tops in popularity with the bicycle ride close behind. Also popular with the sightseers are the scenic trails on Mackinac, many of which can be seen biking or walking as well as by horse.

Boating at "The Crossroads of the Great Lakes" is popular and the Michigan State Waterways Commission provides a yacht harbor for the convenience of the boaters.

Swimming, tennis, and golf, as well as good dancing and other evening entertainment are available.

Fort Mackinac cannon look down on the Trinity Episcopal Church and the Straits of Mackinac.

This Jesuit Mission has been constructed in Marquette Park by Mackinac Historic Parks.

MACKINAC ISLAND CARRIAGE TOUR

The sightseeing tour offered by **Mackinac Island Carriage Tour Corporation** includes the following points of interest which are described by the driver-guide:

VISITOR CENTER Once a United States Coast Guard Station the Visitor Center is provided by the Mackinac Island State Park to provide information about the Park and Island. They also have restrooms.

MARQUETTE PARK A Statue in Father Marquette's honor dominates the center of the park directly below Fort Mackinac. Once a garden for the soldiers at the Fort the park was celebrated by the Daughters of the American Revolution as Michigan's Most Historic Spot.

McGULPIN HOUSE One of Mackinac's oldest, notice its log construction.

JESUIT MISSION This birch bark chapel is constructed in the manner of the Indians of this region. Wax figures inside depict Father Marquette preaching to the Indians.

EPISCOPAL CHURCH The church was built in 1882.

BEAUMONT MEMORIAL This building, restored by the Doctors of Michigan, honors Army Surgeon William Beaumont who made medical history on this site with his digestive experiments

UNITED STATES POST OFFICE Mackinac has its own zip code - **49757** There is no mail delivery on the Island.

STUART HOUSE Built 1817 by the Astor Fur Company as a home for their Mackinac representative. It was refurbished in 1997 by the City of Mackinac Island as museum of the fur trading days.

The Stuart House, built as the Clerk's quarters, has been refurbished recently and is operated as a museum of Astor Fur Trading Days by the City of Mackinac Island. The wheel, that was used to lift furs to the warehouse is on display and is of particular interest.

JOHN JACOB ASTOR HOUSE The original headquarters of the John Jacob Astor fur empire. After the decline of the fur trade it was used as a hotel for many years. It now is refurbished (1996) and contains the Mackinac Island Community hall, some City Offices and artifacts of the fur days.

MACKINAC ISLAND TOWN HALL This is on the site of the original Mackinac County Courthouse which burned.

MACKINAC ISLAND FIRE HALL Home of some of the few motorized vehicles on the Island

LENOX HOTEL Once a resort hotel it now provides housing for Carriage Tour drivers.

BENJAMIN BLACKSMITH SHOP Robert H. Benjamin started the shop in 1884 when the Grand Hotel was being built. His son Herbert continued the business for more then 60 years.

BIDDLE HOUSE Mackinac's oldest house, a museum.

MACKINAC ISLAND MEDICAL CENTER Doctors and nurses provide year around service to residents and visitors There is an ambulance for emergency use.

Home of JOHN BACKHOUSE ASTOR
The Lilacs here are hundreds of years old.

LITTLE STONE CHURCH This Union Congregational Church was built in 1904. Regular Sunday morning services are held at 10:30 AM each Sunday Memorial day to 1st Sunday in October. The church is open daily to visitors.

GRAND HOTEL The world's largest summer hotel overlooks the Grand Hotel swimming pool and formal garden and the Straits of Mackinac.

GRAND HOTEL GOLF COURSE There are nine holes here, The Jewel, and the Grand Hotel has another nine, The Woods, located on top of the Island where they operate the Woods restaurant.

CARRIAGE TOUR BARNS The world's largest horse and buggy barns

SURREY HILL MUSEUM Carriages of the by-gone days are on display here.

The R. H. Benjamin and Son Blacksmith shop at the end of Market Street before it was given to the Mackinac Historic Parks in 1968 and moved to their property on the other end of Market Street. The horses wait to be shod and their old horseshoes added to the pile growing higher by the door. Herbert Benjamin, the Son, corked the shoes during the winter months in order that they would be ready for the busy summer season. Before they were nailed onto the horses foot, they were heated and fitted to the individual horse.

Herbert Benjamin and his father Robert H. Benjamin opened a blacksmith shop on Mackinac in 1884 just before the Grand Hotel was built. While Robert became Postmaster of Mackinac and Sheriff of Mackinac County, Herbert operated the shop for many years. The shop was donated to the state park after Herbert Benjamin's death in 1967 and was moved to its present location.

Private carriages, like this one, are still to be seen on Mackinac, although the costumes of today are slightly different then those in this photo.

CEMETERIES The Catholic and the Protestant Cemeteries have some very old graves as does the Soldiers Cemetery. All are located in the center of the Island. The latter was laid out after the Battle of Mackinac in 1814.

The Island has long been a burial place for Indian chiefs and in years past it was common to see a small group of Indians arrive by canoe with their solemn burden. They would speak to no one but disappear into the center of the Island to return and depart as mysteriously as they had arrived.

SKULL CAVE Where fur trader Alexander Henry hid from Indians after the 1763 massacre.

ARCH ROCK The arch, 149 feet above sea level, can be viewed from the top or from the Lakeshore Drive below.

NICOLET WATCH TOWER If you go up the stairs at the left of the arch you find a tablet to Nicolet the first white man to visit Mackinac. The view here is spectacular.

SCOUT BARRACKS Each week during the summer a troop of about 100 scouts act as a Governor's Honor Guard. They raise and lower flags and act as guides in the Fort, and in other Historic Building on the Fort ticket.

FORT MACKINAC Many of the original buildings from 1780 still stand. The exhibits in the Fort, entered through the Avenue of Flags, depict life on Mackinac in the early years. The exhibits have been developed extensively since 1958 when an admission charge provided funds for their development. There is a lunch room in the Fort and you can walk down from here or come back out to a passing carriage

GOVERNOR'S SUMMER RESIDENCE Michigan Governors spend considerable time here during the summer months.

You can end your tour here and walk down the Fort Hill (to your left) or continue on to town by carriage.

Visitors to Mackinac find that the flags on these poles designate the information booth where they can purchase Carriage Tour tickets, a good way to see some of the sights and enjoy some of the sounds of Mackinac.

A Guide
Walk or Bike
at
MACKINAC ISLAND

You can follow the Lakeshore Drive the 8 miles around the Island. You can walk or ride a bike. If you go east (to your right as you leave the docks) you will see:

Carriage Tour Ticket Office One way to see the Island is to take the Carriage ride. Tickets are available here for the Surrey ride.
Chamber of Commerce Mackinac Island information is available here including maps, hotel rates etc.
Restrooms The City of Mackinac Island operates these behind the Chamber of Commerce building.
Marquette Park In the center of the park is a monument to Father Marquette which was dedicated in 1909. This is a good place to picnic or just sit and enjoy the view. There is playground equipment in the far corner of the park.
Hourly Carriages for Hire At the corner of Marquette Park you can rent a carriage by the hour.
Visitor Center The State Park Visitor Center has rest rooms, Mackinac Publications and information about the Park and Mackinac Island. Eighty percent of the Island is State Park. This building was formally a United States Coast Guard Station.
Indian Agency House Built by an act of Congress, used as a school for many years, it was restored in 1966 and is now part of the State Park. Your State Park ticket will admit you here
Mackinac Island Yacht Dock Provided by the Michigan Waterways Commission it has been enlarged a number of times to accommodate the visiting yachts. In July the Port Huron to Mackinac and the Chicago to Mackinac sail races crowd it with about 300 sail boats.

Mackinac Harbor, at yacht race time in July, is crowded with as many as 300 sailing yachts. Fort Mackinac is in the background.

Mackinac Island Yacht Club A private facility across from the Yacht dock.

Ste. Anne's Catholic Church The oldest Ste. Anne's parish in the US (1695). The present building was built in 1873. It was refurbished in 1996. A museum under the porch tells about its early days.

Old Mission Church This building was erected in 1830 in connection with the Mission House, a school for Indian children. The church has individual family pews and is used now only for occasional weddings arranged thru the State Park.

Mission Point Resort Built by Moral Rearmament and later occupied by Mackinac College and now refurbished as a Hotel.

Continuing east on the Lake Shore Boulevard, now designated as highway MI-185 you come to:

Dwightwood Spring A natural spring named for Dwight Hulbert Wood of Flint, Michigan who sacrificed his life for his brother August 12, 1905 . It was presented to the State by Edwin O. Wood. The stairway here goes to the top of Arch Rock.

Arch Rock Here you can look up at the arch formed so many years ago by the receding glacier waters.

Nature Trail & Walk A State Park facility provides a quiet look at Mackinac woods.

British Landing State Dock Building materials for the maintenance of the State Highway that circles the Island and other projects are brought in here.

British Landing In 1812 the British landed here and transported their canon to Fort Holmes, on the heights.

Ste. Anne's Catholic church was refurbished in 1996 and is a center for Mackinac activities during the winter months when most of the tourists have departed Mackinac Island.

behind Fort Mackinac which allowed them to capture the Fort without firing a shot. The Americans landed here two years later in an effort to recapture but were ambushed. There are restrooms here and **Nature Center**.

If you turn up hill here you can see:

Battle Field This is the site of the Battle of Mackinac 1814 when the Americans attempted to recapture the Island. It is now the location of the
Wawaskamo Golf Club A nine hole course open to the public.
The Woods The upper 9 of the Grand Hotel Golf Course.
Mackinac Island Airport The airport provides a connection to the mainland when the boats are unable to negotiate the ice fields of the Straits of Mackinac. It is open all year and has a lighted runway.
Cave In The Woods A natural limestone formation reached near the airport and near **Crack In The Island**
Pontiac Lookout & Fort Holmes Located above the Cemeteries these hills provide an overview of the Island and surrounding waters to the south over Fort Mackinac and the Light House in the Straits, while Point Lookout provides a view to the east over **Sugar Loaf Rock**. This is especially nice when the Fall colors are dominant. The Les Cheneaux Islands are in the distance.
Pontiac Lookout Located above the Grand Hotel on the west bluff this lookout provides a spectacular panorama of the Straits including the **Mackinac Bridge**. It is named in recognition of Pontiac a great Indian leader and strategist who conspired with nine Indian tribes to overthrow the British domination throughout the Great Lakes.

Cruise ships, shown here have long disappeared from Mackinac. The white sails drying from the yacht race are spread on the grass to dry.

If, at British landing you continue on the Lakeshore Drive you will see:

Brown's Brook This natural spring is a beautiful spot for a picnic along the west side of the Island. No fires or camping are permitted on the Island.
Chimney Rock A Limestone rock formation resembling a huge chimney may be seen above the shoreline.
Lover's Leap This limestone pillar rises to a height of 145 feet above the water. An Indian legend, which gives it its name, says that an Ojibway maiden watched from this height the departure of her lover with a war expedition across the lake. She came day after day to watch for his return and finally when the war party returned without him she cast herself from the cliff.
Devil's Kitchen This natural limestone formations a great picnic spot but climbing here is dangerous.
Board Walk The walk extends from just below the Grand Hotel to the Iroquois Hotel. A great place for sunset watching. No bikes please.
Mackinac Island School This electrically heated school serves the Island for grades K thru 12. There are about 100 students.

Continue along the Board Walk to Town. To walk, on Mackinac away from the busy main street is to discover more of the beauty of the Island.

A favorite walk takes you to:

Cass Monument & Anne's Tablet Walk to **Marquette Park,** across the grass to Father Marquette's Statue, continue diagonally to the playground in the corner of the park and enter the path there that goes up the hill. Its fairly steep and there are a number of stairs at the top. **Cass Monument,** in Memory of Governor Louis Cass, Michigan's first Governor, is by the road at the end of the path. After you have seen the Monument and enjoyed the view of the Straits of Mackinac, take the trail that rises steeply to the

In the early 1900's there were at least 3 of these ice boats. They would race the 20 miles to Cheboygan, with the right ice conditions, in less than 20 minutes. Pat Doud had one of them and Robert Benjamin also had one for transportation.

left as you reached the top of the stairs, and follow it along the bluff a short distance to **Anne's Tablet.**

Continue along the path which brings you behind **Fort Mackinac.** Visit the Fort, there is an entry fee, or pass on to the Governor's residence. Here go down the hill to town or go behind the Gulf course to descend by the Grand Hotel to town.

If you are still ambitious, you are on top of the hill, and you could visit other sites before returning. From the Fort you can follow the signs to: Skull Cave, Cemeteries, Point Lookout, Fort Holmes, Sugar Loaf, Arch Rock Robertson's Folly, the Annex Cottages, or the Airport. If you get lost go down hill to the water and proceed to town.

Point Lookout & Fort Holmes These are located above the cemeteries on the top of the Island and command a view of the Straits area.

Sugar Loaf is below Fort Holmes and stands nearly 100 feet high. In Indian mythology this was the wigwam of the great Spirit Manabozho, who created the world after the great deluge.

The North American, docked at Mackinac awaits its passengers as they tour Mackinac Island.

The Mackinac Bridge is one of the longest in the world. It spans the Straits of Mackinac between the Upper and Lower Peninsulas of Michigan

The original Block Houses at Fort Mackinac continue to guard the Fort but they also welcome thousands of visitors to learn some of the history of Mackinac, Michigan and the United States.

A new era of Lake travel has begun recently with the advent of foreign cruise ships operating on the Great Lakes. This ship anchors in the harbor and brings its passengers in to tour the Island in small boats holding 80 people.

Where to Take Pictures at Mackinac

The horses and carriages at Mackinac Island lend themselves advantageously to photographs by both amateur and professional photographer. The variety of horses, carriages, harness, and backgrounds provide unlimited pictorial subjects.

Early spring brings out the symphony of greens occasioned by the varieties of evergreens as well as the new leaves of the hardwoods.

Summer introduces the hasten and hustle of the horse and buggy, the many geared bikes, and smooth sailing yachts as well as the passage of the lake freighters and picturesque passenger ships.

Fall brings another color creation as the greens give way to the warm reds and yellows but always with the blues of the water and sky.

Winter introduces the quiet solitude of its white splendor as the Straits freeze and the snowmobiles become evident as they replace the horses of summer.

The clear air of Mackinac with the many reflecting surfaces of white and hued buildings and sparkling water create exposure problems to be considered by the photographer. Beautiful compositions can be found most everywhere on Mackinac's Historic Landscape

Bicycling is popular and necessary on Mackinac where there are no cars.

Winter on Mackinac can be exciting! You might see a deer or fox cross the ice from the main land. You might see a Coast Guard ship lead an Ore Freighter through the solid ice of the Straits. Or you might just enjoy the silent stillness of a sleigh ride through the white trails of the Island.

Things to do at Mackinac Island

BICYCLE A number of bike rentals to choose from are located on main street and at some of the hotels. You can get both tandem and single models, with big 'n small tires.

CARRIAGE RIDE Take a taxi or a Tour.

DANCE nightly during the season with music at a number of the hotels and bars.

DRIVE-IT-YOUR-SELF Hire a carriage with a single horse and drive yourself to Mackinac's scenic spots. If you get lost the horse knows the way back.

DINING There are fine restaurants and hotel dining rooms to fit any pocketbook.

HORSE BACK RIDING Fine liveries have horses to suit your taste and riding skill.

HAY RIDE Two horses, and a big wagon and you're off for a great time. Make your arrangements before hand with a dray person but plan it for night or day.

HOURLY CARRIAGE These can be hired by the hour with driver.

PICNIC You can picnic in Marquette Park, along the shore or any place in the State Park. For safety, no fires are allowed.

SWIMMING The Lake is cold and rocky with dangerous currents and deep water but the Hotels have pools for your convenience.

TENNIS There are public courts behind Fort Mackinac and the Grand Hotel courts are open to the public for an hourly fee.

WALK Take long ones or short ones. You can't get lost on Mackinac for long. It isn't big enough and its always down hill to the beach.

One of the large sail yachts racing from Chicago crosses under the Mackinac Bridge. Photo by Thomas Benjamin

CHRONOLOGICAL TABLE

1634 Jean Nicolet. First white man visits Mackinac.
1654 Two French traders pass Mackinac Island.
1665 Father Claude Jean Allouez, a Jesuit Missionary visits Mackinac Island.
1668 New France was divided into provinces, one of which was Michilimackinac.
1670 Mackinac area ceded to France by Indian treaty. Jesuit Father Dablon establishes mission on Mackinac Island.
1671 Father Marquette founded the first mission at St. Lacrosse.
1677 Lilacs are introduced to Mackinac Island by French.
1679 LaSalle visits Mackinac with the first sailing vessel the "Griffin".
1685 Michilimackinac is military center of the Northwest Territory.
1694 Cadillac commands French post at Michilimackinac. In 1701 he founds Fort Ponchartrain, Detroit.
1714 The Fort at St. Ignace was established and garrisoned.
1721 Father Charlevoix visits Mackinac Island.
1761 English troop garrison Michilimackinac.
1765 Major Robert Rogers commands Fort Michilimackinac.
1779 Major Sinclair assumes command of Fort Mackinac and moves the Fort to Mackinac Island.
1763 Massacre at Old Fort Michilimackinac during the conspiracy of Pontiac.
1796 First United States troops occupy Fort Mackinac.
1802 Rev. David Bacon is first Protestant to visit Mackinac.
1808 John Jacob Astor founds The American Fur Co.
1810 Astor Company builds fur warehouse at Mackinac.
1812 Fort Mackinac captured by the British.
1814 Americans attempt to recapture Mackinac Island.
1815 Mackinac repossessed by American troops.
1817 Mackinac Island incorporated as a village. Stuart House built by Astor Fur Company.
1819 First steam boat "Walk in the Water" visits Mackinac.
1822 Dr. William S. Beaumont conducts experiments in digestion on Alexis St. Martin.
1823 First Protestant Mission established by Rev Ferry.
1834 J. T. Astor retires from the American Fur Co.
1837 Michigan becomes a State.
1842 American Fur Company closed here.
1850 James Jesse Strang was crowned King of Beaver Island.

The Grand Hotel since its inception in 1887 has been enlarged a number of times. The Dan Musser family, present owners, continually make improvements to its many facilities.

1854 Fishing Industry replaces the Fur Trade.
1861-65 Civil War
1875 Mackinac Island becomes 2nd National Park.
1887 Grand Hotel is opened as "Plank's Gland Hotel".
1895 Mackinac Island becomes a State Park. United States Troops are removed from the Fort.
1898 Chicago to Mackinac sail races begun.
1909 Father Marquette's Statue was dedicated.
1916 United States Coast Guard Station is built.
1931 D.A.R. designates Mackinac Island as Michigan's Most Historic Spot.
1941 Astor Fur Post restored.
1945 National Governors conference was held at the Grand Hotel
1948 Mackinac Island Carriage Drivers incorporate. New Light house in the middle of Straits is built
1951 Vice President Barkley attends convention of Michigan Democratic Party at Grand Hotel.
1954 Beaumont Memorial dedicated by Michigan Doctors.
1955 Former President Harry S. Truman speaks at Grand Hotel.
1958 Fort Mackinac reactivated with museums and period settings.
1959 Primitive Jesuit Mission built. Biddle House restored by Michigan architects.
1962 Roman Catholic shrine of St. Ann's dedicated.
1965 New enlarged airport dedicated. Enlarged yacht pier dedicated by Michigan Waterways Commission.
1966 Mackinac Island State Park restored Indian Agency House. Moral Rearmament Association opens Mackinac college.
1970 Benjamin Blacksmith Shop given to Mackinac Historic Parks and restored by them on Market Street.
1971 Rex Humbard purchases Mackinac College Buildings
1972 Mount Humbard open for skiing.
1975 President Ford visits Island.
1977 Mackinac College Buildings opened as Inn of Mackinac
1995 State Park celebrates 100 years.

Fort Mackinac visitors before 1900.

Reading List

- Altrocchi, Mrs. J.C. *Wolves Against The Moon.* McMillan 1940.
- Andrews, Roger. *Old Fort Mackinac On The Hill Of History.* Herald Leader Press 1938.
- Armour, David. *100 Years at Mackinac.* Mackinac State Historic Parks 1995.
- Bailey, Lt. Col. John R. M.D. *History of Mackinac.* 1895.
- Baird, Elizabeth Therese. *Reminiscents of Early Days of Mackinac Island.* 1898.
- Blackbird, Chief Andrew J. *History of the Ottawa And Chippewa (O-Jib-Way) Indians.* 1887.
- Block, C. G. *Above Below.* Book Concern, Hancock, 1952.
- Bloomfield, Louis. *The Midwest.* Riverside Press, 1947.
- Bowen, Dana Thomas. *Lore of the Lakes.* 1969.
- Bowen, Dana Thomas. *Memories of the Lakes.* Cleveland Ohio Freshwater Press, Inc., 1969.
- Bowen, Dana Thomas. *Shipwrecks of the Lakes.* 1952.
- Cameron, Frank. *Above Mackinac.* Cameron & Co. with text by Phil Porter, 1994.
- Derleth, August. *Captive Island.* Aladdin Books, N.Y. 1952.
- Fasquelle, Ethel L. *When Michigan Was Young.* Edman, 1950.
- Ford, R. Clyde. *Sandy MacDonalds Man.* A Tale of The Mackinac Fur Trade, Michigan School Services, Inc., 1929.
- Fox, Frances Margaret. *Nancy Davenport.* Rand McNally, 1928.
- Fuller, Iola. *The Loon Feather.*
- Garth, David. *Fire On The Wind.* 1951.
- Hubbard, Gurdon S. *Sketch of Life.* 1802-1886.
- Hunt, Mabel Leigh. *Michel's Island*, Frederick Atokes Co. NY, 1940.
- Johnson, Ida M. *The Michigan Fur Trade.*
- Kelton, Dwight H. LLD. *Annals of Fort Mackinac.* 1882 and 1895.
- Knoblock, C.G. *Above Below.* Book Concern, Hancock, 1952.
- McKee, Russell. *Mackinac–The Gathering Place.* Michigan Natural Resources, 1981.
- Martin, John B. *Call It The North Country.* Knopf, 1944.
- Newton, Stanley. *Mackinac Island and Sault Ste. Marie.* Soo News.
- Petersen, Eugene. *Mackinac Island–Its History in Pictures.* Mackinac Island State Park Comm.
- Orr, Myron D. *Citadel Of The Lakes, Mackinac Island.* Dodd Mead, 1952.
- Orr, Myron D. *Mission to Mackinac.* Dodd Mead, NY, 1956.
- Orr, Myron D. *The Outlander.* Thomas Bouregy, NY, 1959.

Devils Kitchen, on the west side of the Island beyond the Boardwalk has always been a perfect spot for a picnic. The bikes and horses are still popular with residents and visitors alike.

- Page, Lorena M. *Legendary Lore of Mackinac*. 1901.
- Parkman, Francis. *Conspiracy of Pontiac.*
- Porter, Phil. *View From the Veranda*. Mackinac Island State Park Commission.
- Ratigan, William. *Soo Canal.* Eerdman's Publishing Co., Grand Rapids, 1954
- Ratigan, William. *Straits of Mackinac* Wm. B. Eerdmans, Grand Rapids. 1957.
- Reimann, Lewis C. *Between The Iron And The Pine*. Edward Brothers, Ann Arbor, 1951.
- Richardson. M.A. *Eight Days Out Mackinac & The Soo*, Charles R Kerr 1895.
- Roberts. Kenneth. *Northwest Passage.*
- Rubin, Lawrence A. *Mighty Mac* Wayne State U Press, 1985.
- Schoolcraft, Henry *The Writings of Henry Schoolcraft Indian Authority on the L'Arbre Croche Area.*
- Stanley, George M. *Pre-Historic Mackinac Island.* Michigan Dept. of Conservation, Geological Survey Division, 1945.
- Strang, James. *Ancient & Modern Michilimackinac*, Wellman Press, Lansing, 1959.
- VanFleet, Reverend J. A. M. A. *Old And New Mackinac*. 1870.
- Wickman, G. H. *Mackinac Under Three Flags*, 1929.
- Williams, Rev Meade C. *Early Mackinac*. Duffield, 1901, 1919.
- Wood E.O.LLD. *Historic Mackinac*. McMillan, 1918.
- Woolson, Constance Fenimore. *Anne.* Harper, 1882.
- Wright, John C. *The Crooked Tree, Indian Legends of Northern Michigan. C. Fayette Erwin, Harbor Springs, 1917.*

Where the Indians ventured on the Great Lakes and the Straits of Mackinac to trade, today the thousand foot ore carriers slow as they pass the Island. In this way they salute the waters that have been traveled by such a variety of ships through the past centuries. The Straits are a burial ground for many ships that have not survived the angry waters of fall and winter.

Index of Names and Places on Mackinac Island